My Big Book of

Weather

Simon Adams

Created for Kingfisher Publications Plc
by Picthall & Gunzi Limited

Author: Simon Adams
Consultant: Ron Lobeck
Editor: Lauren Robertson
Designer: Floyd Sayers
Illustrators: Mike Saunders,
   Roger Stewart

KINGFISHER
Kingfisher Publications Plc,
New Penderel House,
283–288 High Holborn,
London WC1V 7HZ
www.kingfisherpub.com

First published by Kingfisher
Publications Plc 2001
First published in paperback 2003
10 9 8 7 6 5 4 3 2 1

1TR/0403/WKT/MA/128KMA

A CIP catalogue record for this book
is available from the British Library.

ISBN 0 7534 0815 5

Printed in China

Contents

What is weather?

Earth is wrapped in a thick layer of air called the atmosphere.
This air is made up of gases and it can be hot or cold, wet or dry, and can move fast or stay still. The changes in the air closest to Earth are known as the weather. The Sun's rays keep our bodies warm. Clouds keep us cool by day and warm at night. Winds blow the clouds around the sky. And rain helps plants to grow, and fills our rivers and lakes.

The atmosphere

High above Earth, the atmosphere stretches 800km into space. Scientists have divided it into five invisible layers. These layers are made up of a mixture of gases, such as oxygen and nitrogen. We use satellites in the highest layer to take pictures of the weather from above. Experts on the ground can then tell us what the weather will be like in the next few days or weeks.

Satellite

Exosphere
This layer lies 700–800km from Earth. It is made up of thin gases that drift off into space. This is where satellites orbit our planet.

Space shuttle

Thermosphere
This layer lies 80–700km from Earth. It is the hottest part of the atmosphere, where aurora lights appear and meteorites burn out.

Aurora lights

Shooting stars

Mesosphere
The mesosphere is 50–80km from Earth and is the coldest part of the atmosphere.

Weather balloon

Aeroplane

Stratosphere
This layer is 12–50km above the ground. Aeroplanes fly in the thin air of the stratosphere.

Clouds

Troposphere
The troposphere is up to 12km above the ground and this is where all our weather happens.

A weather satellite takes photographs of the weather from space.

Cloud formations are easy to see from space.

How weather is made

The weather is created by a mixture of water, heat and air. The Sun heats up the air, which makes it move. This moving air is called wind, and it carries heat and water vapour, which is an invisible gas. Clouds, rain, snow and fog are made from water vapour.

Walkers stand on a hillside watching the weather change

Weather and us

The weather affects our daily lives, so we are told by scientists what it will be like in the days ahead. This is called weather forecasting. The study of the weather is called meteorology, and the scientists who do this are called meteorologists. They use temperature, wind speed, air pressure measurements and satellite photographs to forecast the weather.

Light helium gas lifts a weather balloon high into the atmosphere so the instruments it carries can record the weather

Cameras in weather satellites take pictures of weather formations

Watching the weather

Weather stations on land and at sea, aeroplanes, weather balloons and satellites in space are all used for watching and measuring weather. They help scientists to make a weather forecast.

A thermometer measures temperature

An anemometer records wind speed

Weather aeroplanes are used for watching the weather from the sky

A barograph - a type of barometer - keeps a record of changes in air pressure

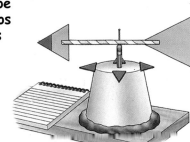
A weather vane shows wind direction

Weather maps show weather formations

Weather stations at sea record changes

Weather power

The weather can be used to make energy that does not cause pollution. Heat from the Sun can drive a car or warm a house. Wind power turns wind turbines to pump water. Without the weather, we could use only oil, coal and gas for our power, and these fuels may run out.

Solar panels on a house use heat from the Sun to heat water and provide warmth

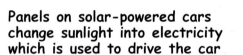

Panels on solar-powered cars change sunlight into electricity which is used to drive the car

Giant wind turbines produce electricity

Studying the weather

The speed of the wind, the temperature of the air, and the amount of rainfall can all be measured using simple equipment. You can note down what type of weather happens at the same time each day, and see how the weather changes over time.

School students studying the weather

Weather through the ages

Earth's weather is always changing, and these changes affect all living things on Earth. Thousands of years ago, cold periods called ice ages or glacials covered the Earth with ice. Warm periods, called interglacials, turned parts of the planet into desert. Today, we are living in an interglacial period.

The dinosaurs may have died out because they could not breathe when volcanic dust filled the air

Weather and extinction

Some types of animals and plants can survive when the weather changes suddenly, but others die out, or become extinct. Scientists believe that the dinosaurs were killed by a sudden change in the weather millions of years ago. Some think that the dust from an erupting volcano filled the sky and turned the Earth dark and cold. Others believe that the dust was caused by a meteorite hitting Earth.

Woolly rhinoceros

Sometimes scientists travel to the coldest places on Earth to carry out research on the weather

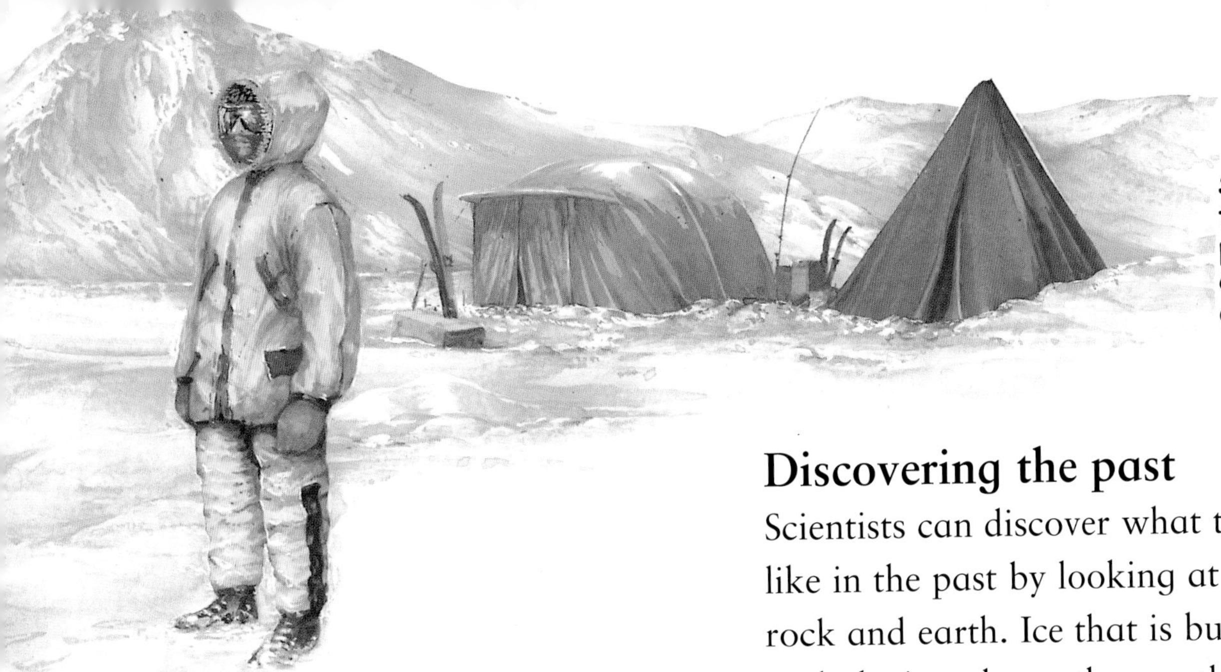

Meteorologists use special equipment to core the ice for samples

Discovering the past

Scientists can discover what the weather was like in the past by looking at samples of ice, rock and earth. Ice that is buried in ice caps and glaciers shows the weather conditions at the time that the ice was created, even if it was formed thousands of years ago.

Ice age world

Ten thousand years ago, Earth was much colder than it is today and looked quite different. Large sheets of ice covered one third of the planet. Mammoths and other animals that lived at that time were covered with thick hair to keep out the cold.

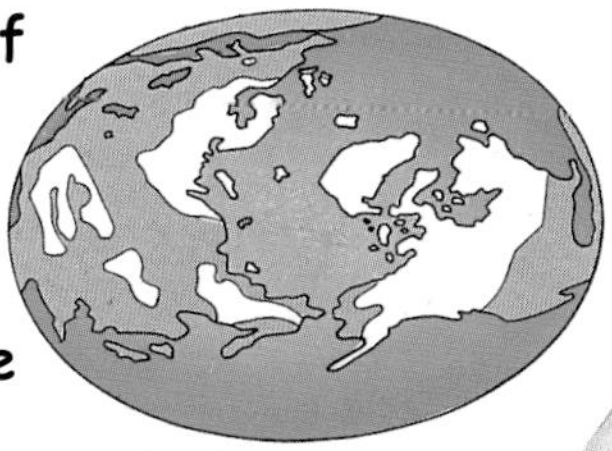

Many areas of land on Earth were covered with ice during the recent ice age

Reindeer

Woolly mammoths

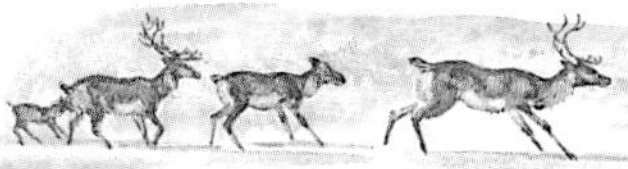

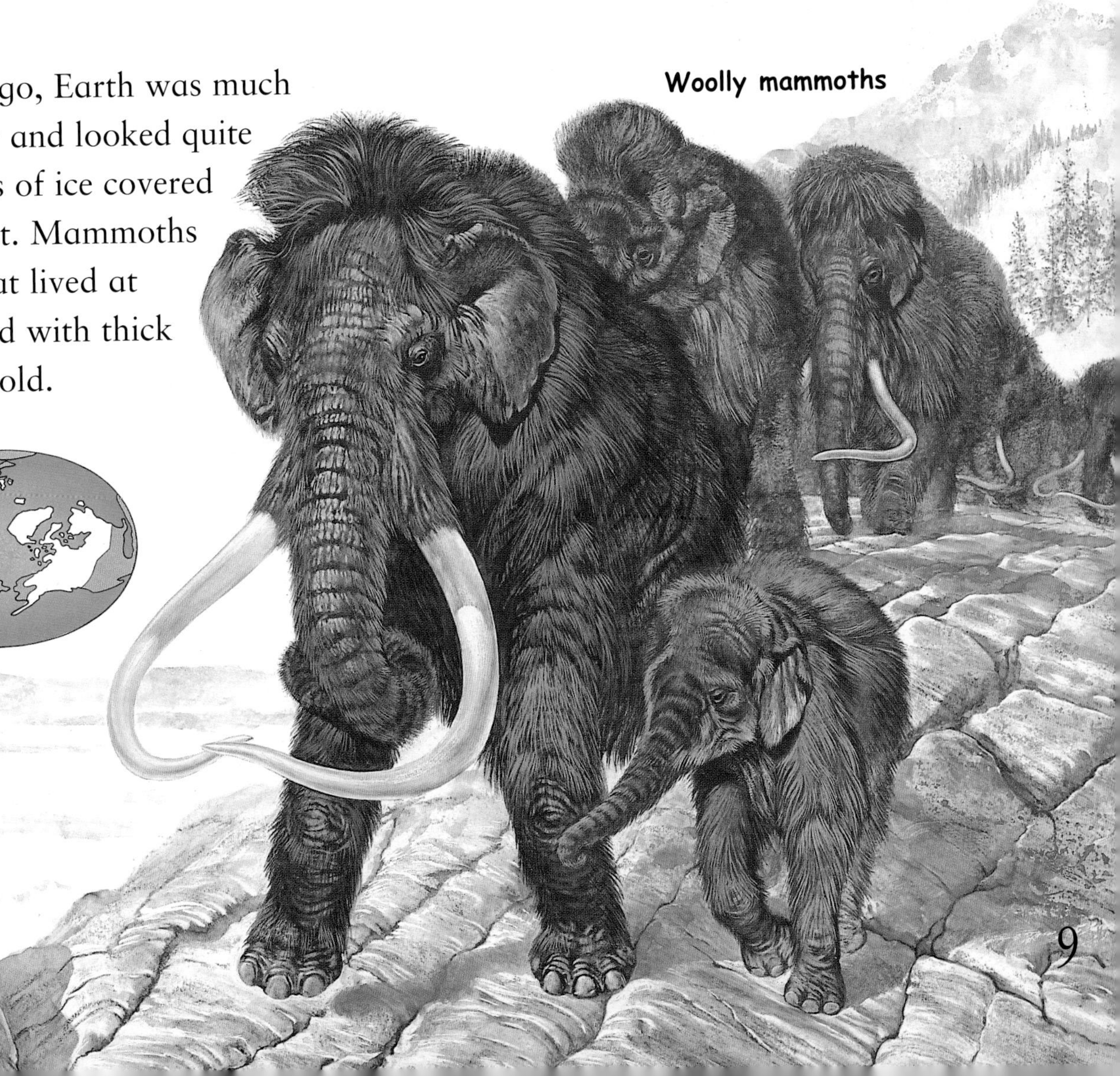

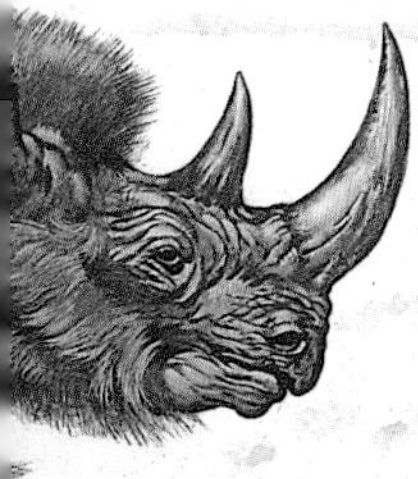

Climate and seasons

The usual weather pattern in a country is called its climate. Different areas of the planet have different climates – some places are mostly hot or cold, and others are usually wet or dry. The weather changes throughout the year, and these changes are known as the seasons. Most places have four seasons, but some have only two.

North Pole

Sun's rays

South Pole

Hottest and coldest

The climate is hottest at the Equator and coldest at the North and South Poles. This is because more of the Sun's rays reach Earth at the Equator than at the Poles. In the mountains and by the sea, the climate is cold. Away from the coasts, it is often hotter and drier by day, but colder at night.

Life at the South Pole is cold and icy

A tropical rainforest is warm and wet

Many desert areas are hot and dry

Different climates

The polar climate – at the North and South Poles – is very cold. Near the Equator, the climate is hot and is described as tropical or Equatorial. In between the Poles and the Equator is the temperate zone. This is either warm or cool, depending on the time of year.

The changing seasons

Seasons change during the year. When it is winter in the northern part of Earth, or northern hemisphere, it is summer in the southern part, or southern hemisphere.

Monsoon winds bring heavy rain that floods parts of Asia

Spring

Spring is the season when the days grow longer and warmer. Nights are cold and the weather may change frequently.

Summer

Summer is the hottest season of the year. The Sun is high in the sky, the days are long and there may be thunderstorms.

Autumn

The nights get longer and the days shorter in autumn. The temperature cools down. It is often misty and the ground may be frosty.

Wet and dry seasons

In East Africa, India and South East Asia, there are only two seasons – the wet season and the dry season. In the wet season, the air is humid and monsoon winds blow in from the sea, carrying heavy rain. In the dry season, monsoon winds blow cool, dry air from the land out to sea.

Winter

Winter is the coldest season of the year. The Sun is low in the sky and the days are short. Snow can fall and ice form in the cold nights.

11

The power of the Sun

Life on Earth would not exist without the Sun's warmth and light. As Earth spins every day on its axis, the side that faces the Sun warms up in the daylight. The side that is hidden from the Sun cools down in the darkness. The change in temperature causes winds to blow, clouds to form, and all other types of weather, such as snow and rain, to develop. It can also lead to floods or droughts.

Too much Sun
People enjoy playing in the Sun and sunbathing in hot weather. But harmful rays from the Sun can burn the skin and cause skin diseases.

Huge clouds form in the Sun's heat, and hurricanes, cyclones and typhoons flare up in the tropics.

Winds from the west, called westerlies, blow on either side of the tropics.

Clouds around the Equator show that Earth's winds meet in this area.

Sun energy

The Sun affects all our weather. Its heat makes water evaporate, or change into a gas, to form water vapour. The heat also makes the water vapour rise and form clouds. In the tropics, the heat of the Sun stirs up moist sea air and creates storm clouds. The Sun also makes the wind blow by heating the air and changing its temperature and pressure.

The Sun's rays travel to Earth 150 million km away

The Sun's heat makes water from the ocean evaporate and form clouds.

The Earth from space

Drought

Many hot parts of the planet have long periods with no rain, and this can cause droughts. The heat makes rivers dry up and kills plants. Cracks appear on the land and crops cannot grow, so people do not have enough food to eat.

When the wind blows

Air presses down on us all the time. Cold, heavy air sinks and creates high pressure. The heavy air warms up and keeps the weather fine. Warm air is light, so it rises and creates low pressure. As it rises, new air blows in to take its place. This is called wind. The weather in low pressure conditions is usually wet and windy. Winds can be soft and gentle, or fast and strong.

Beaufort Scale

The Beaufort Scale was invented by an English admiral, Sir Francis Beaufort. The scale measures how strong the wind is, from force 0 to 12.

1 In forces 0–3, there is no wind or only a light breeze. Clouds drift slowly and the sea is flat or calm.

2 In forces 4–7, the wind is stronger. Trees sway in the breeze and the sea is choppy with waves.

3 In forces 8–12, the wind is fast and powerful. The sea is rough with big waves.

The Coriolis effect

Earth spins on its axis like a top, so the air that moves across the planet flows in a curve. This is called the Coriolis effect. Air moving from the Poles to the Equator curves to the west. Air moving from the Equator to the Poles curves to the east.

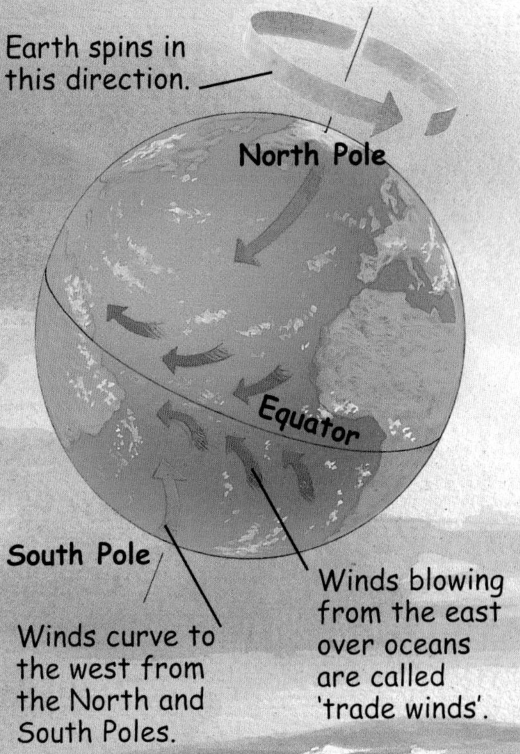

Sails full of wind

Many people enjoy sailing in a yacht or dinghy. The wind blows the sails and drives the boat forward. Sailing boats also have engines so that they can move when there is no wind.

Earth spins in this direction.

North Pole

Equator

South Pole

Winds curve to the west from the North and South Poles.

Winds blowing from the east over oceans are called 'trade winds'.

Wind makes waves form on the sea

A world of water

The air is full of water vapour gas that has evaporated from the seas and lakes. As the water vapour cools, it forms droplets of liquid water. These droplets join together and float in the air as clouds. As the water droplets get bigger, they can form huge, dark rain clouds that become heavier. They then fall to Earth as raindrops. Clouds disappear after it has rained because all the water in them has fallen to Earth.

The water cycle

Air can soak up and let go of water like a sponge. This means that the water on Earth is always being recycled. The Sun's rays heat seawater and it evaporates to become clouds. These clouds then release raindrops. The rainwater drains back to the sea along streams and rivers to begin the water cycle again.

Vapour cools and forms clouds.

Seawater evaporates in the Sun's heat.

Rainwater flows back to the sea along rivers.

Types of rain

Rain is drops of water falling to the ground from clouds. Small drops are known as drizzle. Larger raindrops fall in showers, and a heavy fall of rain is called a downpour.

Drizzle is small drops of rain falling in a soft spray. There is often drizzle when it is foggy.

A short fall of rain is called a shower. After a shower, the sky clears up and the Sun shines again.

A downpour is a heavy fall of rain. The sky is full of dark rain clouds, and puddles form.

Water evaporates from seas, lakes and rivers.

Rain clouds release their heavy load of water droplets.

Rain falls as snow on high areas of land.

Electric skies

Electrical thunderstorms are often exciting but can also be scary. Loud rolls of thunder can be heard many kilometres away from the heart of the storm. Lightning flashes explode from the clouds and light up a dark sky. Fork lightning is filled with electricity that is created in huge, black cumulonimbus clouds. This electricity flows down to Earth, sometimes damaging buildings and trees. Heavy rainfall or hailstones usually add to the drama.

Tree struck by lightning

How distant is a storm?

We can tell how far away a storm is by counting the seconds between the flash of lightning and the clap of thunder. Three seconds equals one kilometre.

When lightning strikes

Lightning is electrical energy, so it is hot and powerful. Its power lasts only for a few millionths of a second, but it is enough to blow a tree apart or topple a tall chimney.

The power of lightning

A thunderstorm can be violent and buildings are often hit by lightning. Many buildings have metal strips, called lightning conductors, inside them. These lead the electricity from the lightning safely down to Earth.

All fogged up

Fog is a cloud that forms on the ground. It looks like smoke, but it is actually tiny drops of water that hang in the air. When it is foggy, it is difficult to see things around you, and driving can be dangerous. A thick fog can stop aeroplanes from taking off and landing. Most forms of transport have to travel very slowly in a fog.

Smog in the city

A thick fog mixed with car exhaust fumes and chimney smoke is called 'smog'. Most cities have smog and the pollution can make people ill. Many countries are trying to reduce the amount of smog, by banning the use of coal fires in the home, for example.

In thick fog, boats cannot be seen, so they use lights or fog horns to warn other boats that they are on the water

A misty morning

Early morning fog on the ground is called mist. It forms after a cool, calm night. When the Sun heats up the air, the mist clears away. After cold nights, tiny drops of water can form on cold blades of grass. This is called dew.

Early morning mist on a meadow

Fogging up the river

Air is full of water vapour. When warm air cools, the water vapour forms a cloud of water droplets. If this happens near the ground, fog or mist is formed. Fog often forms over cold seas, rivers and lakes, as it has on this river in South East Asia.

Fun in the snow

Snow forms high inside clouds when the temperature is low. It is made of tiny crystals of ice. Raindrops often start to fall as ice crystals, but melt on the way down to Earth. In cold weather, ice crystals reach the ground as snowflakes. A heavy snowfall covers the ground like a thick, white blanket. Frost and ice also form when the weather is very cold.

Snow magic

Snowflakes appear to be round and white as they fall. But each one is actually a beautiful ice crystal with six sides. Like people, no two ice crystals are the same.

Icicles form on roofs

Ice rinks are made of ice that is hard and slippery enough to skate on

Snowmen and snowballs are made of wet snow that has stuck together

Ice crystals

In warm weather,
the snow on the top
of a mountain can
melt and tumble down
as an avalanche

Snow-packed
slopes are perfect
for ski-ing

Packed snow is
smooth and slippery
enough for sledging

Frosty windows

When the weather is very
cold, water vapour in the
air freezes into different types
of frost. Frost can form thick
ice on the ground or it can
make patterns on glass (right).

The wildest weather

When thunderstorms happen near the Equator, they can be wild and dangerous. Sometimes storms build up over warm, tropical seas and join together to form hurricanes. These storms are also called typhoons, or tropical cyclones. Hurricane winds reach speeds of up to 360km per hour. Some of these storms can be 800km wide and 15km high. They create huge waves out at sea that flood the land.

Eye in the centre of the storm

Clockwise direction of a cyclone

Typhoons, hurricanes and cyclones spiral anti-clockwise in the Northern Hemisphere and clockwise in the Southern Hemisphere

Twisters

Huge pillars of spiralling air sometimes form beneath thunderclouds. These are called twisters, or tornadoes. Low air pressure inside the twister acts like a giant vacuum cleaner, and sucks up the air around it – as well as anything that it passes over. The winds spinning inside a twister can move at speeds of up to 400km per hour.

Tropical storms

A hurricane, typhoon or cyclone is a violent storm. These storms are made up of a spiral of fast-moving wind around a calm centre called the 'eye'. The storm brings heavy rain as well as strong winds. When hurricanes hit the land, buildings are destroyed, trees are uprooted and people can lose their lives.

Palm trees bend easily in the wind so they do not often break or become uprooted

Spectacular skies

For most of us, the weather does not change much from day to day. Some days are bright and sunny and some are cloudy or rainy. But our skies can surprise us. Rainbows appear after rain and, in certain parts of the world, the night sky can light up with coloured lights called auroras. During a violent thunderstorm, large lumps of ice may crash down to Earth from the sky. These can damage crops, dent cars and break windows.

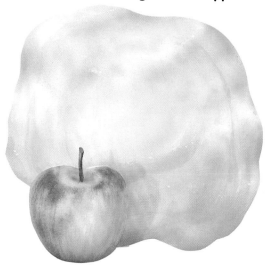

Raining ice

A hailstone is a lump of solid ice made inside a thundercloud. As it moves around in the cloud, it collects water droplets, which then freeze. The hailstone grows heavy and drops to Earth. Most hailstones are about 1cm across.

Colours in the sky

In the Arctic and Antarctic regions, the Sun's rays sometimes meet gases in the thermosphere, and we see a colourful light show in the sky. Bands of red, green and yellow lights fill the night. These are known as the aurora borealis (northern lights) in the northern hemisphere, and the aurora australis (southern lights) in the southern hemisphere.

Rainbows

A rainbow is caused by sunlight passing through millions of raindrops in the sky. As rays of light pass through the water droplets, they are broken up into seven colours – red, orange, yellow, green, blue, indigo and violet. The colours are always the same and appear in the same order. You can only see a rainbow when the Sun is behind you.

Rainbow after a storm in Africa

Climate in crisis

Since the last ice age, the climate on Earth has been getting warmer. In recent years, changes have happened more quickly. Because more coal and oil have been burned, the level of carbon dioxide in the atmosphere is increasing. This stops heat from escaping into space, and Earth is getting warmer. This 'greenhouse effect' is damaging our planet. We must stop polluting the atmosphere if we want to save Earth!

Acid rain

Pollution from factories mixes with water in the air and creates acid rain. This rain destroys plants, eats away at buildings and kills river fish. Acid rain is carried by wind and causes damage over a wide area.

Rising sea levels

Many scientists believe that air pollution is causing the planet's temperatures to rise. Over the next 50 years, Earth may get so much warmer that ice at the Poles will melt, and the sea levels will rise and flood the land.

Glossary

acid rain Rainwater that is full of pollution, which makes it acidic. Acid rain causes damage to trees, crops and buildings.

air pressure The weight of air on the surface of Earth, measured with a barometer.

anemometer An instrument used for measuring wind speed.

atmosphere The air that surrounds Earth. It is made up of a mixture of gases, including nitrogen, oxygen and water vapour.

climate The normal weather conditions that happen in a place over 30 years or more.

condensation The change of a gas into a liquid, such as water vapour into droplets of water.

desert An area of land where less than 25cm of rain falls every year. Deserts can either be hot or cold.

drought Long periods of time when little or no rain falls.

Equator An imaginary line round the centre of Earth.

evaporation This happens when a liquid changes into a gas – i.e. when river water, heated by the Sun's rays, becomes water vapour.

fog Water droplets in the air that make it difficult to see.

fuels Substances, such as coal, wood or petrol, that we burn to make power. Among other things, this power can be used to heat our homes.

greenhouse effect Gases such as carbon dioxide build up in the atmosphere and stop heat on Earth from escaping into space. This raises Earth's temperature and causes the 'greenhouse effect'.

high pressure When the weight of the air on Earth is high.

humid The weather is humid when the air is moist, or damp.

hurricane A violent, tropical storm that brings wind and rain. A hurricane can also be called a typhoon, or a tropical cyclone.

lightning Electricity that has built up inside a cloud and then jumps to Earth in a bright flash.

low pressure When the weight of the air on Earth is low.

meteorite A chunk of rock that crashes to Earth from space. Most are small, but some are big and can cause huge explosions.

mist Water droplets floating in the air. Mist is similar to fog but it lies closer to the ground.

monsoon A wind that blows off the sea on to the land for six months, and then blows the other way for six months.

northern hemisphere The half of Earth north of the Equator.

Poles Points at the top and bottom of Earth. The North Pole is in the Arctic region, and the South Pole is in the Antarctic region.

pollution Poisons in the environment that make us ill.

sea level The normal height of the surface of the sea.

season A period of weather lasting three or six months.

southern hemisphere The half of Earth south of the Equator.

Sun The star at the centre of our solar system, which Earth moves around, or orbits.

temperature The level of hotness of a body or substance.

thermometer An instrument that is used to measure temperature.

tornado A column of wind that spirals from the ground up to a thunder cloud. Also called a twister, or a waterspout at sea.

trade winds Winds that are always blowing over the oceans.

tropics The hot regions of the world around the Equator.

water cycle When water moves from rivers to the air and back to the land as rain.

water vapour Water in the form of a gas floating in the air.

Index

The Romans in Britain

Oil lamps such as this one were everyday articles for Romans in Britain.

This beautifully preserved coin is dated from around AD 140, the same date that the Antonine Wall was built in Scotland by Antoninus Pius. The coin is a sestertius and shows emperor Antoninus Pius who reigned between AD 138 and 161 – immediately after Hadrian.

Many interpretations

This book describes some of the things that happened a long time ago. Very little remains of these times and so much of what is said has, of necessity, to be interpretive. In this book the author has tried to present the generally accepted view of historians.

▲ A small perfume bottle, made of Roman glass.

⚠ Look after our heritage!

It is easy to talk about looking after the environment, but we each have to help. Help is often small things, like being careful when you walk around old buildings, and not leaving scratch marks on anything that you visit. It doesn't take a lot of effort – just attitude.

Curriculum Visions

Curriculum Visions is a registered trademark of Atlantic Europe Publishing Company Ltd.

There's more on-line

There's more about other great Curriculum Visions packs and a wealth of supporting information available at our dedicated web site. Visit:

www.CurriculumVisions.com

✦ Atlantic Europe Publishing

First published in 2004 by
Atlantic Europe Publishing Company Ltd.
Copyright © 2004
Atlantic Europe Publishing Company Ltd.

Reprinted in 2005

Author
Brian Knapp, BSc, PhD

Editor
Robert Anderson, BA, PGCE

Art Director
Duncan McCrae, BSc

Designed and produced by
EARTHSCAPE EDITIONS

Senior Designer
Adele Humphries, BA, PGCE

Printed in China by
WKT Company Ltd

The Romans in Britain – *Curriculum Visions*
**A CIP record for this book is
available from the British Library**

Paperback ISBN 1 86214 401 X
Hardback ISBN 1 86214 403 6

Illustrations (c=centre t=top b=bottom l=left r=right)
Kevin Maddison pages 1, 7, 8–9, 20, 24, 33tr, 40, 42; *Mark Stacey*
cover, pages 6, 12, 13, 14, 16, 17, 26, 32b, 35, 36, 38, 41, 43;
David Woodroffe pages 11, 15, 22, 23, 25, 29br, 30t, 32t, 39, 44.

Picture credits
All photographs are from the Earthscape Editions photolibrary except the following: (c=centre t=top b=bottom l=left r=right)
© *Peter Froste/Museum of London* page 30; © *Reading Museum Service (Reading Borough Council). All rights reserved.* Pages 3cr REDMG:1995.4.1 Euterpe; 3br REDMG:1995.4.1 Silchester Eagle; 3tr REDMG:1962.185.1 Moulsford Torc; 6t REDMG:1995.4.2 Silchester Horse; 34 REDMG:1995.1.103 Silver Spoon; 35tl REDMG:1995.81.31 Samian Ware Bowl; 38cr REDMG:1995.3. Plough share/tip; 39cl REDMG:1995.3. Sheep sheers; 39tr REDMG:1995.3. Roman sickle artefact; 1bl, 45tl REDMG:1995.1.20 Roman writing left behind on a tablet; *Painting by Alan Sorrell © English Heritage Photo Library* page 28b; *Painting by Alan Sorrell © St Albans Museums* page 28–29t; © *Richard Sorrell/Museum of London* page 18–19b.

Acknowledgements
The publishers would like to thank the following for their kind help and advice: *English Heritage, The National Trust* and *Dr Charles Schotman.*

This product is manufactured from sustainable managed forests. For every tree cut down at least one more is planted.

Contents

▶ A beautifully crafted Roman torc made from gold. The Celts too were great craftspeople.

▶ This artefact was found in Britain and would have been owned by a Roman. It is a small bronze statue of a muse, or goddess, called Euterpe. She is the patron of flute playing. Euterpe's religious origins go back even further than the Romans to ancient Greece.

▼ This eagle (shown actual size) was cast in bronze. It would originally have had wings. It shows the fine quality of the casting that the Romans were able to make. Britain's wealth in metals was one of the main reasons that the Romans invaded.

Words, names and places

Words in **CAPITALS** are further explained under 'Words, places and names' on pages 46–47.

The Romans in Britain

This book is about the Romans – a people who lived about 2,000 years ago. The Romans built a vast empire, which for more than 400 years included Britain.

Here is a summary of what happened in Britain during Roman times.

1 About 2,000 years ago the **ROMANS** came to Britain from Italy, a land on the edge of the Mediterranean far to the east of the British Isles. Rome was the capital of the Roman **EMPIRE**.

2 The Romans were one of world's most powerful people. Their strong leaders and well-trained army **CONQUERED** much of Europe and created a great empire.

3 The Romans first sent an army to Britain in 55 BC under **JULIUS CAESAR**, but this army stayed only briefly.

4 A much larger Roman army returned in AD 43 under **CLAUDIUS** and conquered all of Britain. The army was too small to keep control of all the country and it eventually retreated from most of Scotland and built **HADRIAN'S WALL**.

5 The Romans built roads, forts, fine houses and many great public buildings such as temples and **AMPHITHEATRES**.

▼ All civilisations have a way to pay for goods. The Romans used coins as shown below. The Celts had coins, too.

> ### BC and AD
> BC is shorthand for 'before Christ' and indicates that a date is before the traditional date of the birth of Jesus Christ. For example: 55 BC.
>
> AD is shorthand for the latin *Anno Domini*, which means 'in the year of our Lord'. It shows that a date is after the traditional date of the birth of Jesus Christ. For example: AD 55.

As
The Roman unit of currency was the as. This one-as coin shows the Roman emperor Gaius Caesar – better known by his nickname, Caligula. This coin dates from between AD 37 and 41.

Dupondius
Worth two asses. This example shows the emperor Trajan, who ruled between AD 98 and 117. This coin dates from between AD 103 and 111.

Sestertius
Worth four asses. This bronze example shows a portrait of the Roman emperor Hadrian, who reigned between AD 117 and 138. The coin dates from AD 126 to 138.

❻ The Romans made Britain a province (region) of the empire that could supply them with useful goods, such as tin.

❼ Most of Britain's native peoples – we will call them the **BRITISH** – lived in the countryside. The Romans built towns and country houses (**VILLAS**) to live in. The Romans mainly mixed only with the British chiefs.

❽ The Romans never allowed the British to rule themselves. They also sometimes treated the British harshly, and this led to revolts. The most famous revolt was led by Queen **BOUDICCA** in AD 60.

❾ As Roman power weakened at the beginning of the fifth century AD, the Romans began to take their army away. The British were left unprepared to protect themselves against more **INVADERS.**

ROMANS IN BRITAIN TIMELINE

250 BC	Invasion of Britain by Celtic people (**CELTS**) from France.
222 BC	The Romans begin to conquer more land, starting with northern Italy.
218 BC	Hannibal crosses the Alps with elephants.
170 BC	Rome has paved streets for the first time.
146 BC	The Roman empire now includes North Africa, Greece, Spain and France. Some Celts from France (the Belgics) flee to Britain.
55 BC	Emperor Julius Caesar enters Britain.
AD 5	The Romans treat Cymbeline, the king of a powerful British tribe, the Catuvellauni, as king of England, even though he only controls the south.
AD 43	**LEGIONS** under emperor Claudius invade Britain, and defeat the British army under **CARACTACUS** at the Battle of Medway. The Romans found London. The new land (an imperial province) is named **BRITANNIA**.
AD 51	Caractactus captured.
AD 60	Queen Boudicca of the Iceni tribe revolts and sacks London.
AD 78	Roads and forts built in Wales.
AD 82	Roman governor **AGRICOLA** completes the conquest of Britain and reaches northern Scotland (**CALEDONIA**).
AD 87	Scottish Highlands abandoned.
AD 105	Scottish Lowlands abandoned.
AD 122	Emperor **HADRIAN** pulls troops from Scotland and has Hadrian's Wall built across northern England.
AD 140	Emperor **ANTONINUS PIUS** advances back to the rivers Forth and Clyde in Scotland and has the **ANTONINE WALL** built.
AD 163	Antonine Wall abandoned.
AD 180	The Romans are defeated by Scottish '**BARBARIANS**' (**PICTI**) and Hadrian's Wall overrun.
AD 205	Hadrian's Wall rebuilt.
AD 217	Britain peaceful and prosperous to 275 when Saxon raids begin.
AD 287	Carausius, who commands the Roman fleet defending Britain, rebels against Rome and declares himself emperor of Britain.
AD 306	Emperor Constantine supervises the rebuilding of Britain. Peace and prosperity until AD 342.
AD 342	Barbarian attacks become more frequent.
AD 350	Walls are built around many cities.
AD 360	Major attacks by Picti and **SCOTTI** on northern England. These are driven back in AD 370 by emperor Theodosius.
AD 383	Roman legions begin to leave Britain in order to protect Italy from invasion.
AD 410	The Roman emperor Honorius declared to the people of Britannia that they had to "look after their own defence".
AD 425	British have to pay for the help of Saxons, Jutes and Angles from Germany to expel Picti and Scotti (Irish).
AD 457	The British are gradually defeated by the Angles, Saxons and Jutes and many retreat west to Wales. Britain is divided into small kingdoms again.

Front   Back

Denarius
Worth 16 asses. This example is from the time of Julius Caesar and dates from 49 to 48 BC. The front of the coin represents good (the elephant) trampling evil on the back (the serpent).

Aureus
Worth 100 asses. From the period of emperor Claudius from AD 41 to 54.

The British

The British were the people who lived in Britain before the Romans. They were a country people, living close to hilltop forts.

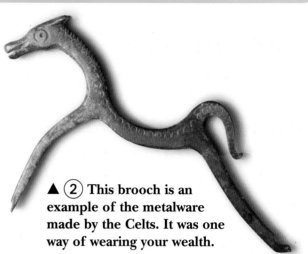

▲ ② This brooch is an example of the metalware made by the Celts. It was one way of wearing your wealth.

◀ ① The relatively simple armour worn by the Celts. Much of it was leather.

The **BRITISH** people who had lived in Britain had been there for hundreds of years before the Romans arrived about 2,000 years ago.

What the British were like

The British, who some people call **CELTS**, were farming people who grew corn and kept pigs, goats, sheep and cattle. Although there were many different **TRIBES** (kingdoms), the people all spoke the same language and shared a common history.

Men or women could become rulers of their tribe. Below the rulers came a small group of nobles. They were warriors whose job was to fight to protect the tribe (picture ①). Some nobles became the tribe's priests and teachers, and were known as **DRUIDS**.

Everybody else worked on the farms, or made pottery, clothing and metal goods. The British did not have slaves. However, in general, not even the nobles could read or write.

Skilled craftspeople

Consequently the British have left little in writing to tell us about their lives. However, we do know that British peoples were skilled in many crafts because, at important funerals the possessions of the dead person were buried with them. Items made of wood and cloth have rotted away, but items made out of metal have survived. This is enough for us to see that the British were very skilled and could make beautiful objects, such as jewellery and swords (pictures ① and ②).

▼ ③ **British, or Celtic, farmhouses were small, round houses with a thatched roof and a fire in the centre. There was just one room, home to a whole family.**

British people built great earthen forts on hilltops. They are called Iron Age forts and are often marked on maps as 'camps'. Here people could live during troubled times. The forts were, however, no protection against the Roman army, as you will see on page 10.

Homes and forts

People normally lived in clusters of small round houses close to their fields and animals (picture ③).

Living in these times was dangerous because kingdoms were often at war with one another.

To protect themselves tribes built large oval-shaped **FORTS** on hilltops. Soil was dug out of the ground to make ditches near the hilltop. The soil was put next to each ditch to make an earth wall. The biggest forts had several ditches and walls. Here the people also kept stores of food.

Although the British fought among themselves, for about 600 years nobody attacked them from overseas. However, this was to change in 55 BC when the Romans arrived!

A hole in the roof let the smoke out

Wooden fences for protection

The Romans

The Romans spread their way of life across their empire. Britain lay on the edge of this empire.

The Romans were a **WARRIOR** people who were always ruled by men. They got much of their wealth by **CONQUERING** other peoples.

▼ ① Ancient Rome was the centre of a very powerful empire and its buildings showed the wealth it had collected from the people and lands it ruled. Roman buildings were similar to those designed by the ancient Greeks. Rome was built on a grand scale. Columns, arches, vaults and domes made the city look impressive.

How Romans gained new land

The Romans kept a large army of paid soldiers (see pages 12 and 13). This was very different from other peoples, who only formed an army when they were attacked. The Roman armies were made of groups of soldiers called **LEGIONS**. The commander of all the legions was the **EMPEROR**.

Because the Roman **EMPIRE** was so large, parts of the empire were ruled by **GOVERNORS**. A governor was put in charge of Britain.

How Romans lived in Rome

Wealthier Romans lived in towns. Here they could go to visit entertainments in a great oval building with tiers of seats called an **AMPHITHEATRE** (pages 36 and 37), or meet and talk in the market-place called a **FORUM** (pictures ① and ②).

▼▶ ② Although ancient Rome has been destroyed and rebuilt many times you can still see many remains today.

Because the army was so important, emperors made sure that the soldiers were well paid. Soldiers were among the wealthiest people in the empire.

The wealthy owned large areas of land in the countryside, called **ESTATES,** and lived in large country houses called **VILLAS** (pages 40 and 41).

The estates were the places where the food was produced. It took many people to grow food, so most lived and worked in the countryside.

The Romans also used **SLAVES**. Slaves were people taken from lands that the Romans had conquered.

Romans bring their way of life to Britain

When the Romans came to Britain, they brought the Roman way of life with them. Wealthy Romans, including retired commanders of the army, lived in luxury in the British countryside. There they built farmhouses which were like the Roman villas in Italy. Others lived in the new towns the Romans built.

Most Romans never intended to settle down in Britain. Although many soldiers married British wives the Romans mostly lived apart from the native British.

The Roman invasions

The Romans wanted the wealth of Britain. However, they did not find the country easy to conquer.

Rome had traded with the British for many years and even the Roman language, **LATIN**, was used by a few British kingdoms on their coins. But on the 26th of August 55 BC the Roman emperor **JULIUS CAESAR**, decided to make Britain part of the Roman empire.

Ten thousand Romans landed near Dover. Some of the British welcomed the Romans and were friendly to them, but others – especially the more powerful tribes – did not want the Romans in Britain and so they fought back.

The British believed their hilltop forts would serve them well against any attack, but they had not bargained for the power of the Roman army. The Romans burned the gates down or surrounded the hill forts, forcing the British to starve or surrender.

The British were soon overpowered and forced to make peace and send a kind of yearly **TAX** called a **TRIBUTE** to Rome.

However, only a year after they arrived, the Roman army left again to fight elsewhere in their vast empire.

▲ ① Claudius ruled the Roman empire from AD 41 to 54.

The return of the Romans

Britain was a country rich in wool, tin and other metals. It could be made to produce a lot of grain. In AD 43 the Roman emperor, **CLAUDIUS** (picture ①), brought a powerful army and called the new colony **BRITANNIA** (picture ②).

Why the British were beaten

When Claudius' army arrived, some of the tribes were friendly, but others were not. Those who decided to fight had little experience at forming large armies and the men were brave, but poorly trained. One of these tribes was led by Caractacus and you can find out about him on pages 14 and 15.

The British only fought when they were not needed on the farms. This made it much easier for the well-trained full-time Roman soldiers to beat them.

▲ ② Britain, which the Romans called Britannia, was on the edge of the Roman empire. It was not particularly important to the Romans and often hard to defend.

The Romans won Britain partly by fighting, but also by showing friendly British leaders that life would be better under Roman rule.

Invasion brings change

As soon as the Romans conquered a region they began building forts, then roads, then towns as each emperor made his mark on the British scene (pictures ③ and ④). These are new to the British way of life.

The purpose of the Roman invasion was to take some of the wealth from Britain back to Rome. But the invasion also brought good things: a better standard of living for many of those nobles who chose to work with the Romans, better education and a more stable country.

▶ ④ Emperor TRAJAN is commemorated with a statue by the Roman wall in London (see page 31).

◀ ③ Emperor HADRIAN, one of the few bearded emperors (see pages 24 and 25).

The Roman army

The Roman army was made of full-time soldiers who were very well trained.

The Roman army was made of multi-skilled soldiers. When they were not fighting, the soldiers built walls and forts, laid out towns, built roads and even became temporary teachers and tax collectors.

Centurions and legions

The Roman army was divided into **LEGIONS** each containing 6,000 men called **LEGIONARIES** (picture ①). Each legion was divided into smaller units of 100 men, each commanded by a **CENTURION** (picture ②).

The Romans also used **AUXILIARIES**. These were soldiers brought from places outside Rome. They were usually led by Romans.

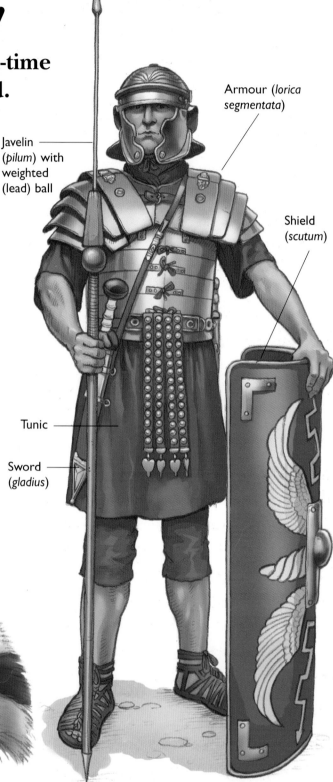

Javelin (*pilum*) with weighted (lead) ball

Armour (*lorica segmentata*)

Shield (*scutum*)

Tunic

Sword (*gladius*)

▶ ② A centurion's helmet. The helmet was made of iron. It had a fan of horsehair across the top and cheek plates down the sides. A metal strap hooked below the chin.

▲ ① The dress of a Roman soldier. The Roman soldier had armour made of metal plates that protected the upper part of the body. Notice the gladius (sword) on the waist belt and the javelin in the hand. The ordinary soldier did not have a fan of horsehair like the centurion.

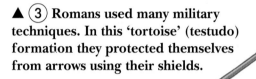

▲ ③ Romans used many military techniques. In this 'tortoise' (testudo) formation they protected themselves from arrows using their shields.

▼ ④ The Romans learned how to attack from a distance using javelins before they used their swords.

Army dress

The Roman soldier wore a woollen tunic that had short sleeves and came down to just above the knees.

To protect himself in battle he also wore a metal helmet and had metal plates protecting his upper body. He carried a wooden shield (picture ③), and he fought with a short sword called a *gladius*, a dagger and one or more throwing spears called javelins (picture ①). The javelins were thrown at the attackers before they got within sword reach (picture ④).

Army pay

The legionary was a full-time soldier and was paid regular wages. He was also paid a share of any spoils from the conquering of new lands.

When he retired, the soldier was given a pension. As a result, being a soldier was a very attractive job in Roman times.

Roman forts

The Romans ruled Britain from **FORTS**. Forts were large and many could house an entire legion (pages 20 and 21).

Inside the fort were stores of food, weapons, a hospital and living quarters for the troops.

The troops sometimes brought their families and these lived in houses just outside the fort walls. There was also an **AMPHITHEATRE** for entertainment and temples for worship.

How big was the army?

For many years the Romans kept an army of 55,000 men in Britain. In the early days they were needed to conquer the country, then they were needed to keep out tribes from Scotland, Ireland and Europe. They called all of the people outside the empire **BARBARIANS**.

Caractacus fights to stay free

Caractacus was a brave tribal leader who resisted the Roman invasion. In the end he was captured by another British tribe.

There were some famous and very brave Britons who did not want to live under the Romans. One of these was called CARACTACUS.

Caractacus led an army made up of people from a number of tribes who tried to stop the Roman invasion (picture ①).

▼ ① Caractacus and his army fight the Romans in AD 43. They soon discover just how well trained and armed the Roman army is and Caractacus is forced to retreat.

The army of Caractacus was made of part-time soldiers who had not trained together. They were no match for the Romans and so they were forced to retreat further and further west. Eventually, the small army with Caractacus had to live in the Welsh hills and could only make hit and run (guerilla) attacks on the Romans.

Caractacus kept up these hit and run raids for nine years.

Early Britain

The Romans did not, at first, mean to capture all of Britain, and to begin with, they advanced only to a line between Exeter and the River Humber. They built a road along this line so that it was easy for their troops to get to places of trouble. They called this road Fosse Way (picture ②) (see page 23).

Advances into Wales

However, Caractacus, along with other tribes in Wales, was still causing trouble along the border, so the Romans decided the only way to deal with the trouble was to conquer all of England and Wales (picture ②). This they did by AD 79.

Betrayed

The Romans still could not capture Caractacus, so they had to make a deal with another of the British tribes called the Brigantes.

If the Brigantes could hand Caractacus over, then the Romans would look favourably on them. So when Caractacus was next in the lands of the Brigantes – who he thought were friendly to him – they captured him and handed him to the Romans.

Courage recognised

The Romans took Caractacus and his family to Rome. Here he expected to be executed. However, emperor Claudius admired his courage and so pardoned him. Nevertheless, they never let him return to Britain in case he might cause trouble again.

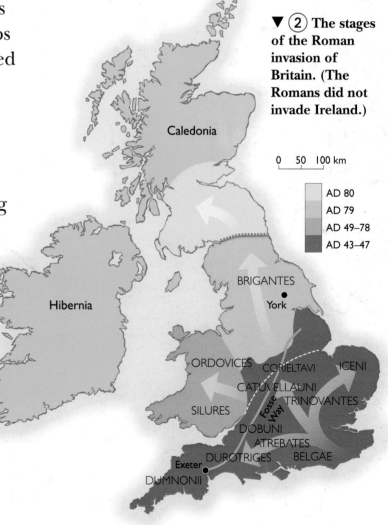

▼ ② The stages of the Roman invasion of Britain. (The Romans did not invade Ireland.)

Caledonia

0   50   100 km

AD 80
AD 79
AD 49–78
AD 43–47

BRIGANTES
York

Hibernia

ORDOVICES   CORIELTAVI   ICENI
CATUVELLAUNI
SILURES   TRINOVANTES
DOBUNI
ATREBATES
Exeter   DUROTRIGES   BELGAE
DUMNONII

Fosse Way

Differing ways of life

The Romans lived very different ways of life and had different beliefs from the British. As a result, there was often an uneasy peace between them.

Britain became an imperial province of Rome and the British were ruled by the Romans.

The Romans and the British were such different people, there were many chances for misunderstandings. Here are some of their differences.

We cannot understand the language the Romans speak. Only a few of us have been taught Latin.

The Celtic view

The Romans think we are second-class citizens.

We have always been ruled by kings and queens. We are loyal to our rulers and we like them to sort out our problems. We have no need for foreign laws and courthouses. We are used to dealing with each problem as it comes up.

We do not have slaves. All of our people are free.

We live in the countryside and have little use for towns.

Our priests are called Druids. If the spirits are angry they will offer a human sacrifice.

We believe our gods are spirits that are everywhere around us. We have spirits in trees, lakes, rivers and mountains.

We have a strict set of rules telling us how to live our lives. It is called the rule of law.

We believe in gods that are like people. Jupiter is the most important god. He is the god of the heavens and responsible for thunder and lightning and other terrible natural events.

Mars is the second most important god. He is the bringer of war. Other important gods are Juno and Minerva, but there are many others.

The Roman view

We think human sacrifice is a terrible thing.

We believe in the rule of law. The British have never had any laws, so we must make them obey ours.

We often make captured people into slaves. How else would we get people to do all of the hard work?

The British are second-class citizens because they have been conquered.

We think that a good way to keep the British peaceful is to make their rulers more wealthy and more like Roman citizens.

Boudicca rebels

Some Britons were treated badly by the Romans and so they rebelled. The most famous was a queen – Boudicca.

The Romans mainly tried to work with the rulers of the tribes they had captured. In this way there was less likely to be trouble from them. However, they insisted that the natives carried no weapons. This was, of course, quite against the traditions of the native tribes.

The Romans also expected to get the lands and money of the British rulers as soon as they died. But this was not, of course, what the family of the rulers expected.

Worst of all, the Romans were not used to dealing with women leaders, as women were not allowed to hold important positions in Rome. In Britain they decided to put up with this difficulty – for a while.

Boudicca rebels

Trouble flared just 17 years after the invasion when the king of the Iceni, a British tribe in the east, died. His wife – **BOUDICCA** (also spelled Boadicea) became queen (pictures ① and ②).

▼ ① Boudicca was a queen of the Iceni tribe. Her fight to stand up for her rights has been seen as a symbol for British people through the ages. They sacked London killing thousands of people and burned buildings as they went.

▼ ② This statue of Boudicca is near the Houses of Parliament in London. She is shown riding a horse-driven CHARIOT into battle. In fact we don't know what Boudicca looked like.

The Romans used the king's death as an excuse to take over the tribe's lands and stop Boudicca becoming queen. Many people in the kingdom had their property taken away and others were harshly treated – especially the women.

In desperation, in AD 60 Boudicca rallied other people whose lands had also been seized and started a REBELLION.

Boudicca attacks

Boudicca chose to wait until the main Roman army was far to the west in Wales, then she launched her attack. Boudicca and her followers advanced through the town of St Albans (then called Verulamium) on to the Roman capital at London (then called Londinium) and burned it to the ground. The rebels killed anyone who they thought was connected with the Romans. In all some 70,000 people were killed by the rebels.

There was never any question of Boudicca winning, or even coming to a peaceable agreement with the Romans. The Roman army slowly but surely took back control. Faced with defeat, Boudicca took poison rather than be captured.

The Roman lesson

The rebellion made the Romans realise that they had to treat the British with more respect. As a result, there was never another rebellion like Boudicca's.

Roman forts

The Romans needed to keep control of the country. They did this by building forts.

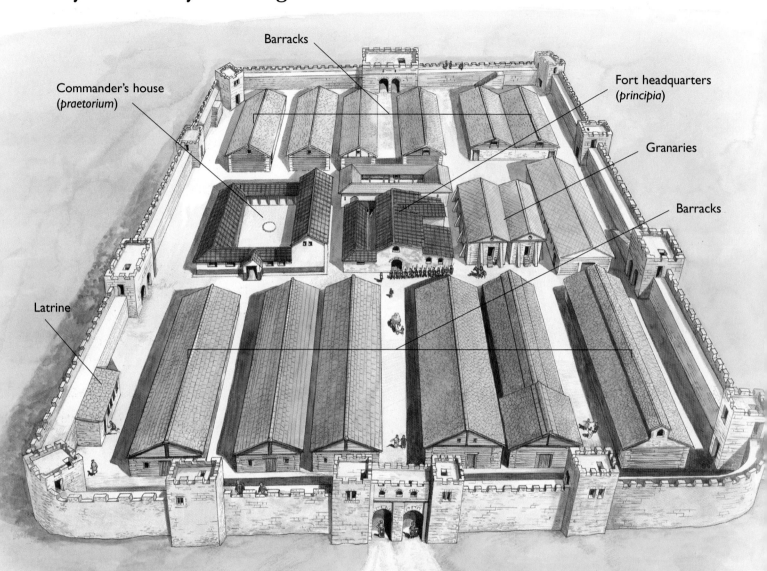

Barracks

Commander's house
(*praetorium*)

Fort headquarters
(*principia*)

Granaries

Barracks

Latrine

▲ ① Roman forts were large rectangles with rounded corners. Their walls were often built of brick or stone. They were intended more as Roman 'police stations' than as places to defend.

The headquarters building (*principia*) the most important building, the commanding officer's house (*praetorium*) and the granaries were in the middle. The front and back areas were used for barracks, hospital, workshops, bakery, stables and latrine (toilet).

▶ ② A general view over Housesteads Fort (Vercovicium – the place of the fighters).

The Romans knew that the key to keeping the British under control was to make sure that they could put down any rebellion quickly. So they built a network of forts across the country (picture ①). A few remain and are among the best preserved of all Roman sites (pictures ② and ③).

How a fort was organised

Forts were places where a large number of troops were based. As a result, they were among the largest Roman structures.

Each wall had at least one entrance, usually a double gateway guarded by towers. Main roads ran between gates, creating a grid-iron pattern of roads within the fort.

The soldiers were housed in barracks. Each barrack block was home to a century (80 men).

The fort needed a supply of water. This was usually obtained by digging a well.

The commander

The commander was one of the few people allowed to live inside the fort with his family. His courtyard house, called the *praetorium*, was the largest building in the fort and much like any civilian villa. The dining area was heated by a **HYPOCAUST** (picture ④).

The commander worked from the nearby headquarters courtyard building called the *principia*. Here were offices and also a **BASILICA**, the Roman assembly hall where the orders of the day were read out.

The men washed themselves in a heated bath house, but they washed their clothes in an open tank of cold water. Their toilet – called a latrine – was near the lowest corner of the fort. If possible, running water was provided to keep the toilet flushed.

▲ ④ The hypocaust (hot air system) under the heated military baths at Binchester, County Durham. This is the best preserved Roman military bath house in Britain.

◀ ③ The stone slab floor of the Roman granaries at Corbridge Fort, Northumberland. The pillars allowed the granary to be ventilated and kept rats at bay.

Roman roads

The Romans knew that, if they wanted to unite a country, the way to do this was to make it easy for people to get about. So they built a network of fine roads.

0   50   100 km

Antonine Wall

Dere Street

Hadrian's Wall

York

Watling Street

Fosse Way

▲ ① Map of Roman roads and main forts. There were many Roman roads criss-crossing Britain. The roads surrounding London were built like spokes of a wheel so that all of the country could be reached from the capital.

The Romans built roads which were almost always perfectly straight. Many can be traced today (picture ①) and in places the original surface can still be seen.

Roads were used for transporting goods such as grain and pottery as well as for the use of the army.

How were the roads built?

The roads were built 8 metres wide, so that columns of troops or carts could pass easily. Each road had foundations made from a strong layer of stones.

The surface was made from well-fitting cobblestones or blocks of stone (picture ②). The roads had a slope to each side (they were cambered) to let the rain run away. On each side there was a drainage ditch.

▶ ② One fine stretch of Roman Road crosses Wheeldale Moor, near Whitby, North Yorkshire.

The road pattern

One of the first roads to be built was called Fosse Way. It runs from south west to the north east and it marks the line the Romans first set up as the boundary of newly captured Britannia (see page 15). Another important road was Watling Street, linking the ports in the south east with the Fosse Way and beyond.

By AD 84 the Roman legions had reached the northernmost part of Scotland. By doing this they brought the whole island of Britain under a single ruler for the first time ever.

To supply the forts in this new area new roads were built.

Dere Street

One of the most important roads was the road to Scotland, we now know as Dere Street (picture ③).

Dere Street was completed about AD 80. It ran from York to a place near to Edinburgh on the Firth of Forth (picture ④).

The road ran through northern England. This was never safe country for the Romans because the local people – the Brigantes – were liable to revolt at any time. To protect Dere Street a line of forts was built.

▲ ③ Dere Street, Binchester, County Durham.

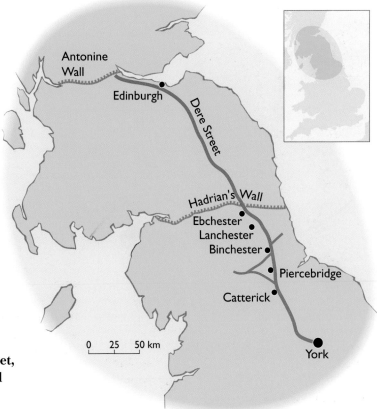

▶ ④ The route of Dere Street, linking York to Hadrian's Wall (Stanegate) and Scotland.

Hadrian and Antonine Walls

As part of their struggle to defend land in Scotland, the Romans built two walls from east to west coasts. They were among the largest structures the Romans built anywhere.

▲ ② The wall and the remains of a milecastle. The milecastle was a fortified gateway through the wall.

By trying to occupy Scotland, the Romans overstretched themselves. By AD 120 emperor **HADRIAN** had a massive problem. He could not afford to keep many thousands of troops in Scotland, yet without troops how was he to stop raids on England by the Scottish Highlanders?

He first tried to make peace with the **CLANS** in southern Scotland. In this way he would have a 'buffer' of people between England and the Scottish Highlands.

Road

Vallum

Milecastle

▲ ① A side view of the wall, road and ditches. The *vallum* was a ditch with two banks. It was a boundary line. No civilian could build a house between the *vallum* and the wall. The *vallum* could only be crossed at forts.

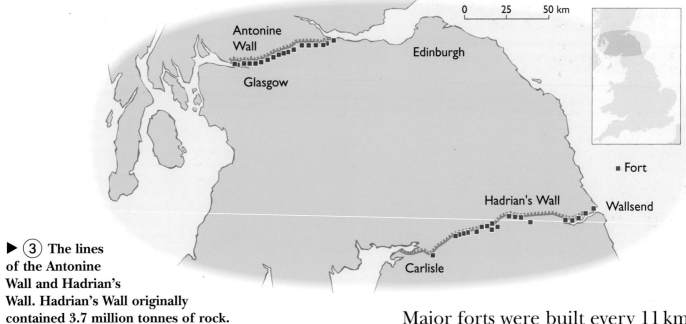

▶ ③ The lines of the Antonine Wall and Hadrian's Wall. Hadrian's Wall originally contained 3.7 million tonnes of rock.

But this was not enough. Eventually he decided to build a massive stone wall from Wallsend, near Newcastle on the east coast of northern England, to the Solway Firth near Carlisle on the west coast (pictures ①, ② and ③). It took six years – from AD 122 to 128 – and it followed a natural wall made by ancient volcanic rocks.

Hadrian's Wall

Hadrian's Wall was nearly 118 km (73 Roman miles) long. It was just under 3 m wide and 4 m high, and made of massive blocks of stone. Behind the wall was a road and a wide ditch and bank complex called the *vallum* (picture ①).

Every 400 to 500 m there was a tower and at every 1,500 m (a Roman mile) there was a small fort called a milecastle (picture ②). Between milecastles there were two turrets.

Major forts were built every 11 km which housed a garrison of up to 1,000 men together with their horses.

Hadrian's Wall was manned until the year 410 – nearly 300 years!

The Antonine Wall

In AD 140, some 20 years after Hadrian's Wall had been built, the new Roman emperor **ANTONINUS PIUS** reached out into Scotland again.

His army advanced to where Edinburgh and Glasgow stand today. Here the distance between coasts is just 60 km. An earth and turf wall was built, which we now know as the **ANTONINE WALL**.

The wall was 3 m high and 4 m wide. It had forts about 3 km apart and a military road behind it. Sculptures were set along its top as a mark of the edge of Roman Britain.

But the Romans could not defend the Antonine Wall and 20 years later the army retreated to Hadrian's Wall.

The Civil Zone

Life was much more peaceful away from the frontier region, or Military Zone. This area was called the Civil Zone.

When the Romans arrived, they had found many tribes who were often at war with one another. Unless they were prepared to keep a large number of troops in Britain, a way had to be found to turn the British into peaceful people.

▼ ① **The Romans introduced the British to a wide range of new goods, and a new way of trading, through shops and markets in towns.**

The areas where people were most friendly to the Romans were the south and east of England. Forts were built at first in this area, but later modified into towns.

The Romans then began to show the leaders of the British how they could become wealthier by trading with them (picture ①).

They were never as successful in the north and west and so the **MILITARY ZONE** was never developed in this way. It remained dominated by the army housed in forts.

Life in the Civil Zone

The first governor to develop the **CIVIL ZONE** was **AGRICOLA**. He did two things. He encouraged the British to adopt a Roman way of life, wearing Roman clothes, building temples, villas, baths, forums (picture ②) and amphitheatres. He also made sure that the sons of the British leaders were educated the Roman way, especially by learning the Roman language – **LATIN** (picture ③).

▲ ② The remains of buildings in Roman towns can still be found, such as here in Chester.

▶ ③ Learning was an important activity – but only for the boys of the wealthy. They wrote Latin using metal spikes (called *stylii*) on wax tablets. This is a picture of a replica.

Many of the words we use today in modern English have their origins in Latin.

As a result, not only did the more wealthy British start to live in villas, but they also began to read and write in Latin. More people could read and write in Roman times than for a thousand years after the Romans left.

The common people

The Romans spent their efforts on the ruling class of the British tribes – the kings, queens and nobles. But Roman ways did not reach the people in the countryside in the same way. Eventually they changed the shape of their houses from round huts to a Roman rectangular design, but they did not learn Latin and they kept on living and farming their traditional way. This was important for the end of Roman times (see page 44) because it meant that, when the rulers went away, so did Roman ideas.

Roman towns

The Romans loved their towns, but towns had a practical purpose, too.

Romans enjoyed living in towns so they could talk with friends and see entertainments. But there was a practical reason to build towns, too. For example, towns were places where Romans collected **TAXES** and had law courts. So, even while they were conquering Britain, the Romans began to lay out towns. Their grand scheme took about a century.

Amphitheatre

▲ ① Roman Silchester (*Calleva*) had the regular plan common of Roman cities. Notice the basilica and forum in the centre, the baths to one side of the centre and the amphitheatre beyond the walls.

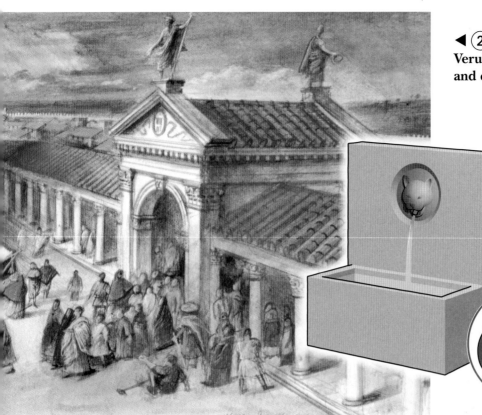

◀ ② This is the main square, or forum, at Verulamium (St Albans) with the law courts and city hall. It is all on a grand scale.

◀ ③ Water was brought into the town in stone channels called AQUEDUCTS and fed to a central fountain or trough. The most important houses would get their own water. It was supplied using lead pipes. The Latin for lead is *plumbum*, and this is how we get the modern word plumbing. Sewage would often be carried away from the public toilets by water, too.

Roman towns

All Roman towns followed the same basic plan (picture ①). First they laid out a criss-cross (grid-iron) pattern of roads covering an area up to 2 square kilometres. Then they planned in important buildings near the centre.

Right at the heart of the town was a meeting and market-place called the **FORUM** (picture ②). Around the outside of the forum were shops and other buildings and a covered walkway held up by columns. On one side of the forum there was a town hall and law courts (called the **BASILICA**). There would also be public baths and clean water supplies (picture ③).

Temples were dotted about across the town, in part because the Romans worshipped many gods and each had to have its own temple.

One public building was too big to fit in the centre of the town. This was the place for entertainment called the **AMPHITHEATRE** (see pages 36 and 37).

Homes

Most of the town was made of houses. The rich and middle classes had houses set in their own large gardens, so the town would have looked more like a collection of houses in the countryside than the sort of town we are used to today. Other people lived in simple homes cramped together and some even lived in blocks of apartments. It was not possible to cook in such apartments and so many Romans ate at 'fast-food' stalls in the markets.

Roman London

London was the biggest Roman town. This is what it looked like.

London was built on a flat piece of dry land by the River Thames. Between this site and the sea were marshes. A tribe of Britons lived at the site, which they called *Llon dyn* (ship hill).

It began as a fort

The Romans quickly set up a fort, then started to use the site as a port, Romanising the Celtic name to *Londinium* (picture ①). This site was a natural meeting place of routes.

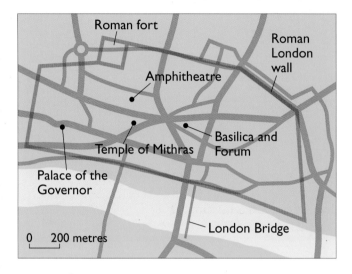

▲▼ ① The map above shows you the main features of London as the Romans knew it. The River Fleet comes in from the bottom and the picture looks south east.

▶ ② Part of the remains of London's city wall. The Roman wall is the lower part, where the red lines are. This was built about AD 200. The upper part was built in the Middle Ages.

   The wall required a vast amount of stone. There is no local stone in London, so only the facings were made from good stone, and the core was filled with a mixture of mortar and rubble.

The Romans built many roads outwards from London. The straight line of some Roman roads, such as Watling Street (now called Edgware Road), show this well.

The first London bridge

The Thames was wider and shallower than we see it today and it could be forded at low tide. But as traffic on the Roman roads increased, they needed to cross at all times of the day, so they built a wooden tressel bridge over the river.

London grows

Because London was at the centre of many roads, it quickly grew into the main city of Britain.

Over a kilometre of waterfront quays were built in brick and stone.

Fine buildings

Over the centuries the Romans put up many fine buildings inside their city. They built the largest basilica outside Rome, a forum, an amphitheatre and baths.

London wall

Much later the town was enclosed within walls seven metres high and two metres thick (picture ②). It enclosed a city of 1.3 square kilometres and housed some 30,000 people. It must have been one of the largest structures in England (except for Hadrian's Wall).

Cooking and eating

Meals were important as time to talk as well as food to eat.

Food was an important part of the Roman day. However, what you ate depended both on how much money you had and what your work was.

◀ ① Roman spoon. The pointed end was used for extracting snails from their shells or marrow from bones.

Soldiers

It was the rule that hard men got hard food. Soldiers' meals were cold bread, porridge, cheese and beans with cheap watered down wine to wash it down. They didn't even get hot food.

Civilians

Poor people might eat one meal a day, while the wealthy would eat three. Breakfast (*jentaculum*) was a kind of snack. A light lunch (*prandium*) often consisted of the leftovers from the night before. The main meal, dinner (*cena*) was in the late afternoon, or near sunset.

Entertaining

While poor people ate their meal on an earth-trampled floor, the wealthy had separate kitchens.

In the centre of the dining room (picture ④) was the table ringed by couches. There was also a sideboard designed to show off silverware. The table held serving dishes and offerings to gods.

Jentaculum – Breakfast
Many poor people ate bread dipped in wine for breakfast. The wealthier used honey, olives and dates.

Prandium – Lunch
This was a snack eaten by the wealthy. It consisted of bread, fruit, cheese, or leftovers from dinner the night before.

Cena – Dinner
Cena could consist simply of vegetables with olive oil for those of the lower class, or a most elaborate several-course meal for the well-to-do (or anywhere in-between, depending upon the circumstances). The typical dinner, however, had three courses.

The first course, the *gustus* was the appetizer course. Mulsum (wine mixed with honey) would be served along with salads, eggs, shellfish, mushrooms and other appetizers.

The second course, the meat course, or *lena*, might provide pork, poultry, fish, game, and/or exotic birds, served with vegetables.

The final course, called the *secundae mensae*, or "second table" was given its name because at dinner parties, the entire table was removed after the first two courses, and a new one put in its place for the final dessert course. This course offered fruits, plain, stuffed and in sauces, honey cakes, nuts and, of course, wine.

The food would often have been garnished with sauces, herbs and spices. A favourite flavouring for all kinds of food was garam – a fermented fish sauce.

◀ ② Pottery brought to the table was in sight of visitors and so was of high quality. This red clay was imported from France (Gaul) and called Samian ware. It was very fashionable among wealthy Romans. The real name for Samian ware was *terra sigillata*, which means "clay with designs pressed onto it".

▶ ③ A fine example of a Roman glass jug.

The quality of the dishes reflected how much money could be spent (pictures ② and ③). There was no cutlery except spoons (picture ①).

▲ ④ Guests were led into the dining room, where the gods were praised. Sandals were taken off and hands washed with water and dried on towels. Each guest brought their own napkin.

Food was brought to them and they ate it while lying down on couches. They did not sit to the table as we do now. Food was mainly eaten with the fingers even by the most wealthy Romans.

Roman leisure

The Romans had many ways of enjoying themselves. Some we still do, others we would now think are unpleasant.

The Romans were not just people who conquered others. They also liked to find time to enjoy themselves. Here are some examples of what they did.

Amphitheatre

The biggest building in a town would be the **AMPHITHEATRE** (picture ①). The word amphitheatre means theatre with seats on all sides.

▲ ② The Romans were fond of watching games where people fought one another. These people were called gladiators.

▼ ① Amphitheatres were often very large and so built just outside the walls of Roman towns. None of these have survived as buildings in Britain, so we need to look at the Colosseum in Rome (shown here) to get an idea of how impressive they must have been. The best preserved amphitheatre foundations in Britain are at Caerleon in Gwent.

This was usually shaped like an oval with tiered seats (much like a football stadium). In the centre, and sunk below ground in a kind of huge pit, was a flat area called the arena. Plays could be performed here. Also **GLADIATORS** would fight one another (picture ②), or they would fight wild animals. Spectators would also watch wild animals fighting each other. Much of this might seem unpleasant to us, but remember that the Romans lived in violent times.

Most amphitheatres would have had an awning, a cloth cover that could be pulled across to keep the spectators dry in case of rain.

Public baths

The Romans liked to bathe, much as we enjoy going to a swimming pool. The public baths (picture ③) contained great communal baths capable of taking hundreds of people at a time.

The baths were enclosed, but around them were gardens for exercise. Baths might be heated by fires, or, in favourable places, hot springs would be used.

People bathed in three main baths: hot, cold and lukewarm. Baths were highly decorated using marble and mosaics. Paintings (called frescos) covered the walls. The main public rooms were also heated by **HYPOCAUST**.

▼ ③ One of the bathing pools at Bath, Somerset.

Roman countryside

The Romans may have preferred towns, but they got their food from the countryside.

The Romans were good organisers. They organised their army and their towns. All of the people in the army and the towns needed feeding, so they also made sure the countryside was organised to feed them.

Farms

The Romans introduced new crops to Britain – ones that would give more variety to their meals. They introduced cabbages, peas and turnips, apples, plums and cherries. They also introduced chickens.

But the Romans also prized natural British products. For example, wool from British sheep was made into rugs and cloaks and sold across the empire.

The Romans did not farm themselves. Most of the land was farmed by the British (picture ①).

▼ ① People cultivated the land by turning it over using a wooden plough pulled by oxen. To protect the cutting tip of the plough from being worn away it was fitted with an iron ploughshare.

This artefact is a type of ploughshare from Roman times.

On the Roman estates (see pages 40 and 41) the land was farmed by slaves brought from overseas.

During Roman times, farming was so successful that there was plenty of surplus food to send to towns. Grain was also sent to the ports for shipping overseas. There was even space for the wealthy to have gardens and to plant flowers.

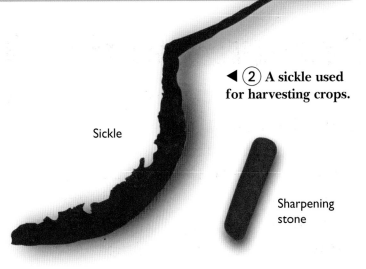

Sickle

◀ ② A sickle used for harvesting crops.

Sharpening stone

Industry

Today we are used to factories and workshops being in towns and cities. But in Roman times this was not the case. Goods were mostly made in the countryside. This was true whether it was the making of iron, the making of pottery or the spinning and weaving of cloth.

Making iron and other metals (pictures ② and ③), or firing pots (picture ④) needed heat and this came from burning wood. Furnaces were built close to forests where the wood could be cut down.

Spinning and weaving were things done by country people when they were not at work in the fields. Mostly they used the wool from their own sheep.

Once made, people would take their metal goods, pots or cloth and sell them in the towns. The towns were therefore important markets for selling and buying.

▼ ③ This metal artefact is a preserved set of sheep sheers. The handle is on the right and cutting blades on the left.

▶ ④ Storage jars – *amphorae* – came in all shapes and sizes. Carrying heavy clay to the cities was difficult and so they were made near clay pits in the countryside. The finished *amphorae* were then transported to towns and cities.

39

Villas

The Romans and wealthy Britons lived on estates called villas. Some were simple, but others were as big as palaces.

Most people lived in small round one roomed thatched cottages with earthen floors (picture ①). These houses were not well made and they did not last long. Even their remains are almost impossible to find today. Only evidence of post holes remains for archaeologists to find.

The more wealthy farmers, however, lived in bigger houses made of stone, brick and tile. This is why there are more remains of wealthy houses than of ordinary farmhouses.

▲ ① Traditional British houses were mainly circular. The Romans introduced rectangular houses. They still had a thatched roof over a single room and a beaten earth floor. There was no chimney.

▼ ② The main house in a villa was made of stone and had many rooms. It had a tiled roof, separate servant, slave and family rooms and was heated by a hypocaust. Most villas were relatively close to towns. Romans did not have estates in remote areas.

▶ ③ The owners lived in rooms with mosaics on the floors. Many mosaics show sea creatures or Roman gods.

Villas

Wealthy Romans and British owned villas. Country villas were estates (large farms) including a farmhouse and other buildings (picture ②).

The farmhouse would be made of stone and the roof tiled, not thatched. The house would even have many rooms. Such farmhouses were often formed around a courtyard, with the inner sides having a verandah and all facing over gardens. The kitchen, bakery, wine press, well and other farm buildings would be nearby.

The main living rooms in the villa were often heated with a **HYPOCAUST**. A slave was needed to keep the fire stoked all of the time. The floors of the main rooms were decorated with pictures made of small pieces of coloured stone. These were called **MOSAICS** (pictures ③ and ④).

▼ ④ The figure of 'Winter' from the dining room mosaic at Chedworth Villa.

Tiles made of glazed or fired clay could take the daily wear and tear and at the same time looked decorative.

The end of Roman times

The Roman influence on Britain lasted for nearly 400 years. But when the emperors became weak, the empire fell apart and the Romans left Britain.

▼ ① The Romans used galleys – ships with oars as well as sails. But they were mostly designed for the calmer waters of the Mediterranean Sea and were hard to handle in the storms of the English Channel.

The Roman empire existed because it had strong rulers and a powerful army.

Britain, as other parts of the empire, needed the army to protect it from invaders and to maintain order.

The Romans had never trained the British to rule themselves, even after 400 years.

Keeping raiders at bay

The Romans had built Hadrian's Wall to keep the Scottish out. But in the 3rd and 4th centuries there were more attacks from Europe.

The Romans may have tried to keep the raiders out by building a series of coastal forts in south east England (known as the Saxon Shore). But they mainly relied on a fleet of warships (picture ①) to capture the barbarians at sea.

The Romans leave

As the Roman empire weakened, raids on the British shores increased (picture ②). By AD 410, the Roman emperor Honorius declared to the people of Britannia that they had to "look after their own defence". The Roman empire was nearly at an end.

▲ ② After the Romans left, their fine houses were easy prey to attacking barbarians such as the Saxons.

The British found it hard to defend themselves once the Romans had gone. They were left in their fine country farmhouse villas and in their walled towns, but they could not defend themselves from raids.

The Angles and Saxons arrive

From AD 425 barbarians from Europe, who we now call the Angles, Saxons and Jutes, as well as the people from Scotland (the **PICTI**) and Ireland (the **SCOTTI**) raided and plundered at will. The Angles (or Engles) would finally give their name to the country called England.

The British tried to pay **PROTECTION MONEY** to keep the barbarians away. Then they had to give away land in exchange for protection. So, in this way, Roman Britain fell apart, the towns were abandoned, and new groups of settlers moved in.

Life in Britain would not be as civilised as in Roman times for more than 1,000 years.

What the Romans left us

The Roman empire collapsed 1,600 years ago. But the Romans brought us many good things. Some still survive.

The Romans left Britain about 1,600 years ago. But while they were here they changed the face of England.

- They introduced public buildings and the rule of law.

- They laid out roads (picture ①) and used a system of measurement – miles – that we still use. The Romans also gave us feet and inches.

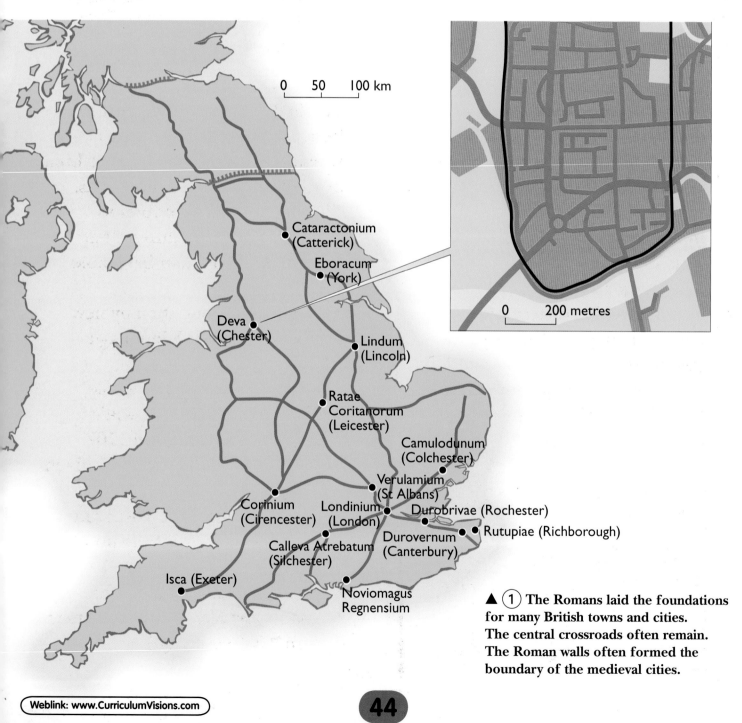

0   50   100 km

0   200 metres

Cataractonium (Catterick)

Eboracum (York)

Deva (Chester)

Lindum (Lincoln)

Ratae Coritanorum (Leicester)

Camulodunum (Colchester)

Verulamium (St Albans)

Cornium (Cirencester)

Londinium (London)

Durobrivae (Rochester)

Rutupiae (Richborough)

Durovernum (Canterbury)

Calleva Atrebatum (Silchester)

Isca (Exeter)

Noviomagus Regnensium

▲ ① The Romans laid the foundations for many British towns and cities. The central crossroads often remain. The Roman walls often formed the boundary of the medieval cities.

◀ ③ The Romans provided many records of their everyday life which is why we have quite good evidence of what they did.

▼ ④ Sage, parsley, garlic and thyme were Mediterranean herbs that the Romans brought to Britain. They were used as herbs to flavour food and as medicines – sage in particular was sacred to the Romans and regarded as a powerful healer. The Romans also brought edible snails to Britain. These still survive today in small colonies.

- They laid out the first towns, some of which have survived at least in plan (picture ①). Most towns which have part of their name as "chester", were towns that grew up in Roman times close to Roman forts (for example, Chester, Manchester, Chichester).

- Roman architecture has been copied throughout history (picture ②).

- The Romans brought Britain the first plumbing systems and the first sewers.

▶ ② The classical building style of Roman times has been copied throughout history. This picture is the Radcliffe Camera (library) in Oxford. The Roman style of building is still used today.

- The first version of the country houses and estates, for which Britain is now so famous, were built by the Romans and called villas.

- They taught British nobles to read and write, something that no British people had been able to do before.

- The Romans brought many new words to the English language (picture ③).

- The Romans united the whole of Britain for a while. It would not be united again until 1707 when Scotland joined with England and Wales.

- Romans brought Christianity to Britain towards the end of their time.

- The Romans brought over many new plants and some new animals (picture ④).

Words, names and places

AGRICOLA A Roman general who made major conquests in Britain, capturing Wales and Scotland. His life is recorded by his son-in-law Tacitus and is one of the main historical sources of life in Britain under the Romans.

AMPHITHEATRE A large oval stadium where tens of thousands of people could be entertained. In the centre was a walled pit called an arena. In many cases amphitheatres were built away from the city centre because they were so large.

ANTONINE WALL A wall built between Glasgow and Edinburgh on the instructions of emperor Antoninus Pius. It is 60 km long and was begun in AD 140.

ANTONINUS PIUS A Roman emperor who ruled from AD 138 to 161.

AQUEDUCT An open channel (canal) that brought clean water to Roman towns.

AUXILIARIES The soldiers of the Roman army who were not citizens of Rome. Most came from the provinces.

BARBARIAN Any person who lived outside the Roman empire. Picti, Scotti and Saxons were all called barbarians by the Romans. Barbarians were thought of as violent and uncivilised people by the Romans.

BASILICA One of the main public buildings in a Roman town where meetings and courts were held.

BOUDICCA The queen of the Iceni tribe in Britain who rebelled against the Romans when the lands of her people were taken away. During the rebellion, which lasted between AD 60 and 61, many people were killed. However, the rebellion taught the Romans to treat the British better.

BRITANNIA The name given by the Romans to the parts of Britain that they ruled; a province of the Roman empire.

BRITISH The people who lived in Britain at the time of the Roman invasion. They were a Celtic people and are therefore sometimes known as Celts.

CALEDONIA The part of Britain north of Hadrian's Wall in Roman times.

CARACTACUS The leader of the main force of British who resisted the invasion by the Romans in AD 43.

CELTS The name for a group of peoples who lived in France and the British Isles at the time of the Roman invasion.

CENTURION A commander of 100 legionaries in the Roman army.

CHARIOT A cart with two wheels pulled by horses. They had been used since ancient times to ride into battle. This is how the Celts used them. The Romans preferred cavalry (soldiers who fight on horseback), but they used chariots for racing around the arena.

CIVIL ZONE The part of Britain that the Romans felt was safe and so did not need a permanent army stationed in it.

CLAN The name for a tribe in which all of the members share common ancestors.

CLAUDIUS Roman emperor from AD 41 to 54 who made Britain a province of the Roman empire.

CONQUER/CONQUERED To successfully invade another country or land.

DRUID A Celtic priest.

EMPEROR The head of an empire.

EMPIRE A very large area consisting of more than one country, and ruled by a single head of state, or emperor.

ESTATE A very large farm.

FORT A strong, well defended place occupied only by troops and surrounded with a ditch, rampart and a wall of wooden stakes.

FORUM A large space in the middle of a town where markets were held. Law courts and other public buildings were built around the sides of the forum.

GLADIATOR A slave trained to fight other gladiators or animals in amphitheatres.

GOVERNOR The ruler of a part, or province, of the Roman empire who carried out the wishes of the emperor.

HADRIAN Roman emperor between AD 117 and 138.

HADRIAN'S WALL A wall 118 kilometres (73 miles) long built by the Romans across northern England between AD 122 and 128. It was designed to keep the barbarians of Scotland away. It was named after the emperor Hadrian.

HYPOCAUST The Roman form of central heating. Hot air was fed under the floors and in the walls of living rooms. It was used only by the wealthy.

INVADERS People who attack another country or land with the intention of taking it over.

JULIUS CAESAR A Roman general who was born about 100 BC and who later became emperor. He was killed in 44 BC.

LATIN The language spoken and written by the Romans.

LEGION The main division of the Roman army and made up of 5,000 to 6,000 men.

LEGIONARIES The soldiers of the Roman army; members of a legion.

MILITARY ZONE The part of Britain where there was a constant need for legions because of the threat from barbarians.

MOSAIC A pattern stuck onto a surface such as a floor and made from coloured pieces of glass, stones, pottery and other materials. Romans were very fond of mosaics as decoration.

PICTI Celtic tribes that lived in Scotland during and after Roman times. Picti means "painted people".

PROTECTION MONEY Money that was paid to possible invaders to keep them away from the country.

REBELLION An uprising within a country by people who think they have been badly treated.

ROMANS A people who formed an empire centred on Rome more than 2,000 years ago. The Roman empire lasted for many hundreds of years and it was one of the greatest empires the world has ever known.

SCOTTI Celtic tribes that occupied Ireland (Scotia) during and after Roman times. Scotti means "people of Scotia".

SLAVE A person who is bought and sold. Most slaves were people from countries that had been conquered by the Romans. Some slaves were treated well by the Romans and could even be given their freedom. Others were treated very harshly. For example, a master had the right to kill his slave.

TAX Money collected by a government. In Roman times, some of the money was used to pay for public buildings, soldiers and road building.

TOGA A loose, cloak-like garment worn by Roman men.

TRAJAN Roman emperor who ruled between AD 98 and 117.

TRIBE A group of people who live in one part of a country and are ruled by a chief. The chief can often be called a prince or a king. When the Romans arrived, the British were divided into tribes.

TRIBUTE A kind of tax that one group of people pay to another, especially by a people defeated in war to the victors.

VILLA A large house and its surrounding grounds. Villas were built in the towns (where the grounds were small) and in the country (where the grounds were a large farm, or estate).

WARRIOR A professional soldier.

Index